THE FACE IN THE WINDOW

THE FACE IN THE WINDOW

poems

Linda Stern Zisquit

THE SHEEP MEADOW PRESS
RIVERDALE-ON-HUDSON, NEW YORK

All inquiries and permission requests should be addressed to:
The Sheep Meadow Press
5247 Independence Avenue
Riverdale-on-Hudson, New York 10471

Distributed by the University Press of New England.
Designed and typeset by the Sheep Meadow Press.

Printed on acid-free paper in the United States. This book meets the guidelines for permanence and durability of the Committee on Production Guidelines for Book Longevity of the Council on Library Resources.

Library of Congress Cataloguing-in-Publication Data

Zisquit, Linda.
The face in the window : poems / Linda Stern Zisquit.
p. cm.
Includes bibliographical references.
ISBN 1-931357-17-X (acid-free paper)
I. Title.
PS3576.I576F33 2004
811'.54--dc22

2004011171

We are grateful to the New York State Council on the Arts, a state agency, for their support.

For Donald

and in memory of my parents

Ann and Gerald Stern

ACKNOWLEDGMENTS

Grateful acknowledgement is made to the following journals in which versions of these poems have appeared:

CrossConnect	"I cannot speak to you"
The Cortland Review	"So the concentrated mourning days," "Why didn't I bring a sweater," "Four weeks have passed now," "Six months before the first stroke"
The Drunken Boat	"Look, he's sleeping now," "I'm not home," "Oh the habit of acquisition," "In the Vitas Hospice House," "Morning again," "She opened her eyes"
Jewish Women's Literary Journal	"He always made a lot of noise"
Kerem	"One day maybe I'll come here," "Dear mother gone into the rocking"
Lyric	"When the sexual life", "In a painting by Francis Bacon"
MAGGID	"K'desha," "Convalescent Home," "Was that you, Ma," "I've invited them all in here," "Airmail"
Natural Bridge	"Picture Window"
Parnassus	"Nineteen lines can't comprise"
Pequod	"Verse," "Snake," "Snow"
Shofar	"Speck," "Orphan," "How to Resist Temptation"
Washington Square	"Feed the Enemy"

With special thanks to Gabriel Levin and Tina Davis Snyder for their generous help.

CONTENTS

1

VERSE

The man speaks to me as
body flesh cunt mouth hole
and liquid all around his
words do lubricate my soul.

Why if 'lady' is ideal do I
respond? if mother's tone
taught me anything, why
do I follow like a hound?

K'DESHA

Once
in burning summer
on a night fierce with sirens
and still air
I let Rachmaninoff
pound the walls and open doors,
I sat on the step and could not
contain the sounds
to obey her, I couldn't stay
inside.
Through the dark
I drove along Buffalo streets
till the blinking strobe-
light of a man's apartment
beckoned, and not sure
of anything but her *don't*,
I parked and stepped off
the hardrock of one life
onto the slope of the next.

K'desha (ke-day-sha): harlot, also the ancient Temple prostitute who engaged with holiness through her sexuality, from Hebrew *kadosh*, or holy (the same root as in *Kaddish*, the mourners' prayer)

PICTURE WINDOW

Pregnant in my mother's house
I suffocated under her roof:
there was no air.
I tried dancing in the dark
reading her look
everything I knew
to put myself somewhere.
I remembered a girl
coming late to the swollen steps
her mother's face pressed against the glass
its perfect vision condemning early
its eyes undoing awaited
doom. Never small losses
a kiss portended ruin:
I came home late, a whore
in my mother's house!
We finished those nights
over double solitaire
without a nod
or a wager to win
or a straight spoken word.

HOW TO RESIST TEMPTATION

Read the notes from the morning's class
on the *Sota*
on the winds of folly
that blow through the secret place
where God is asked to vacate
and no witness sees.
Don't mention it to a soul.
Try to imagine the ink in which all of His Names
are erased
and the swallowing
and the fumes that rise
through the mouth of flesh.
Then take a human step
back.

Sota: the Talmudic Tractate which discusses the adulterous woman

THOSE WITH A SECRET

Those with a secret
the ones who keep shame
in a dark and silent chamber

are the ones who can't stop
talking, all the words
filling the spaces around them,

their holes open but never
empty to receive
what's being offered.

ASHKELON BEACH

If anyone saw they thought I was waving,
a useless gesture easily
interpreted as its reverse. And the voice,

my mouth opening let in floods,
I couldn't scream. I thought the inner
reserves of a past so willed meant

in danger the strokes away would prove
mighty, defeat the waves, and the call
for help would be, above all, heard.

Instead I remained alone, struggling
toward shore as the undertow kept me back
and then pulled me down.

It was close in there,
walls caving in, no sun, no moon,
only a child's face blinking its beacon light.

BLIND

All gates are locked except the gates of wounded feelings.
— The Talmud

The doctor implied
it was her
wanton dance
that sealed
my brother's eye
blind.

And her horror
of that lie
is what loaded the gun
she clutched at night,
pinned her face
to the pane

as she waited
for my
laughter
in the arms of a man,
or the scent of sex
alive
on glistening skin.

1962

You're still looking?
A willynilly search
in the corners of their bedroom:
the stale bathrobe smell
and the growth on his face,
Vitalis in his hair,
she asleep on her side, the nylon
nightgown clinging to her
thigh, and from her nostrils
a dankness.

Did you ever hear them talking?
Some nights I'd hear her climb the stairs,
legs thick after hours ironing.
Folding down the quilted spread
she sighed, how tired she was!
He'd fallen asleep downstairs
snoring in front of the tv,
lying back on the brown
naugahyde barcalounger
covered with her white
wool chinchilla coat
I never saw her wear.
It became what he wore
over him
while he slept days
and she refused to wake him,
as his life swerved
into gambling
lost job
darkness.

Whose rules did she follow?
For some people unhappiness
is a moral obligation.
But I didn't want to touch him then
any more than she did,
rising for work
marching out the door
in the cold early morning
blame
made her strong.

Wasn't there a night
when they held each other
and loved what they had?
I crept to the top of the stairs
and listened.
Stephen came out of his room on tiptoes.
For some reason neither of us
went further.
She sat at the kitchen table
playing solitaire,
the circles under her eyes puffy, huge.
She no longer slept, it seems,
shuffling in her Angel Treads,
waiting for the back door to open—
how could you? she screamed
her dreams, his cowardice!
how could he gamble how
could he
sit night after night
with that scum?
till he was one of them,
the failure, the Willy Loman.

But he didn't answer?
and Stephen and I
flat on our stomachs,
bodies stretched over the stairs,
ears pressed to the blurry
thickness that became our secret.
Not that her voice didn't carry –
no,
maybe we were trying
to hear him.

I thought you hated the sleeping man.
I hated that coat.
One late afternoon Stephen and I
carried it from the den closet
to the car
and drove to the city dump
where we must have stood solemn
and chanted some phrase
in final parting.
Then we flung the coat
high over metal scraps and stinks,
waited to hear it drop.
But it caught on a rusty pole
and stayed there waving-
a banner
over the garbage,
a great bird
flapping its white wing.

FIRST RULE

He'll think
she's thinking
he won't come.

Her mother taught
a lady holds back,
closes when most
he desires.

But defiant
to the end
she grimly
embraces
what breaks
from her arms.

THE DOOR

Not being loved by you
isn't so different from before

when the door opening
meant your hands, your breathing

around me. Because your love
was a light turned inward

and nothing has been extinguished.
Only then like a moon I glowed

and now I'm all a darkness.

NO SIGN

My body moves
through the flame of yours

without a trace of carbon
on my skin, no sign

I burn, no evidence
how flammable

how charred
these sinewy parts are.

CALCIUM

In the back seat of their new Oldsmobile
I sit behind them,
she in her arthritic pain he in his confusion
turns into driveways he doesn't mean to.
Sometimes she forgets her cane as we get out.
I quickly shut my door and reach to help.

We sit on the beach and watch the waves.
I focus my lens and capture her sad face,
his availability. Blood thickens as we age,
plaque fills the veins, the back rounds
like a hill under which a whole life's hidden.

FIRST STEPS

Morning after no sleep,
no floor underfoot.
All the years she held
herself up and he
accompanied her,
I was supported, too.

Now it's over. I worry
about their limbs,
the way they stare,
their hearts pumping,
their clothes
dusty with urine
filling the air.

EMERGENCY

So which one was it,
a visit to the doctor
for Ma's sake
or mine?
So he could yell "Anna"
(not her name
exactly)
and tell her to repeat
"This is a good day!"
so Dad could finally see it
with his own eyes:
her laughter
(inappropriate)
and her stare off?

Dad of course cried
but Ma couldn't say
"Oh, Jerry!"
and be disgusted
in the usual way.
It was puzzling
for the doctor,
this "sudden" decline.
And that's one thing
I was after.

The other, his red eye
swollen or shut
made his face at first
strange
but then I accustomed to it
and recognized

in his pants' drape
and gray and white shirt's
stripe (or blue?)
the man
from an airport dream
pushing me to the wall
pressing against me
his breathing heavy
his eye wandering.

I slump
into his force,
go back and forth
to my life,
my mother's decline
is my entrance into his,
her rescue dependent
on his focus,
my longing for her
is a barren
attraction to him.

THE WORLD MOVING

When the shades are down in my
parents' condo and Mom's retired
to a nursing home, only the neurologist's
blue striped shirt arouses
hope. It's funny in Florida
how fears combine, a day's desires
fall in layers flattened to the past unless
a doctor inspires fantasy. So I let him
take me to the point of thinking he
could save us. But he refused
to treat her at the Rehab Center,
said it's not his territory. I hired a van,
my father raged (why rock the boat?
upset the cart?) at my scheme to wreak
upheaval. All the ride to his office she sat
locked in the wheelchair looking out.
It was the last time she would see
the world moving, the last time I
would turn to him for anyone's arrival.

SPECK

"You don't need a purse!" he'd yell,
"leave it home!"   He carried her tissues
a lipstick her checkbook:
whatever he took over   she gave up.

CONVALESCENT HOME

1

I couldn't sit still when I visited her,
rushing off as if I had an appointment –

now it seems every act was a show.
Even our walks by the canal behind the home

when I wheeled her around and pointed to birds
hovering over the water and named trees,

exotic flowers. I left her in the dining hall
during feedings: a lady among spoons clanging,

bibs on the overgrown kids
who swallowed their carrots and had their chins

wiped clean. I asked if she remembered
the day it happened, when her dying started.

Back in her room, the one with *Annie*
tacked on the door in childish script

I'd read to her, certain she wasn't listening.

2

Once I asked her if I looked the age of the author
and she said the name under the author's photo.

"Mom, you can read?" How little I expected
of her, as though nothing made a difference anymore –

Of course she could read, and looked up at me
quizzically as she used to.

ASHES

I'm small. Why did I think
I was big? That I could fill myself
with the world's *yes*,

look so good in my black dress
that everyone turned to see,
didn't he? And now it's gone,

or rags, or buried in a jar
preserved for one who knows
her size and what clothes are for.

DREAM

Your face was soft, your mouth in place
not fixed in that open howl
I glimpsed from far away down the hall
where you were one of them,
had become a look-alike to every other
angry lost forgotten creature,
your hair combed
yet startling in its shape
as though you slept outside
and couldn't shake off the leaves
or remove the sand the loam
the frost from your scalp.

You said it was okay,
this lasting end,
perpetual solace
of punishing blanks.

You were holding the blanket,
folding and folding
till it became a tiny square
you rocked gently to your chest and cooed,
played peek-a-boo
till it grew and cradled you in its arms.

2

*

I cannot speak to you in the old way,
half truth half hidden, fearing
you're doubting my goodness.
Not because I've finished doubting
myself, and not – the obvious choice –
because I need some open grace
to grow away from you.
Then I lied and bore the fact
with pride. No, you'll never know
what I'm about to tell you:
these months since you died
I've gone back, reread your letters
slowly, one by one,
and the harvest I've reaped
is your goodness, and the sorrow
in the field where I once lay
and now look up to see you gone
is the burnt-out patch when I lacked
sympathy, and let you in half-way.

*

My throat closed in that moment, at first
a tiny irritation forming a film across
the passage where air flows, my mouth
opened for water, I gasped as the coughing
took over, tightening the rope – it seemed
you were there, helpless as never before,
watching my rehearsal of your end in this
room I go to since you're gone, where I turn
to you like a child choking, eyes widening
in disbelief you offer no cure. Then I
swallowed pills, adrenaline frosted my lips,
nothing worked as I expected, nothing
removed the elusive dust-mote gripping
the back of my tongue. What does it mean
to be suddenly impaired, vulnerable to any
wind that sways the branches, afraid some
needle might stick in my pores, cloud
my vision, prick my tender skin? till
like you I am an offering, severed, split?

*

In the dream just before waking I greeted my mother.
She'd come to visit, I was happy, but then
where, in which room would we put her?
The question loomed, we went downstairs
to a basement we don't have here, my husband said
I shouldn't worry, he would fix a good bed for her.
I started cooking and forgot her, preoccupation
my misdemeanor. Then I went looking where
he'd put her, it was perfect, the upstairs bedroom
of our daughter. She was asleep, the covers
over her, thick and soft it made me happy.
When I entered the fan was blowing directly on her.
I only stood in horror as it blew and blew
right on her, she was cold, I knew for certain,
she was blowing like a feather, she was cold and
she was blowing and I must have done that to her,
now I wonder if I saw her could I have stopped
the fan and saved her? She was flying like a feather
that hovers above the water, she was listening
I could see her, she was crying, it was over.

*

Six months before the first stroke she packed
up their belongings, from bedroom to basement
to the attic where she found my love letters
inside the shoe box, my girl scout uniform
folded in safekeeping; she sorted, discarded
and probably stopped to read to see if she could
at last decipher my choices; her silk scarves
stacked in perfect squares inside the painted metal
box, sweaters and nylons, what ladylike bed-things
she could abide, cotton sheets still crisp after
years of laundering. Some furniture she shipped
to me here, overseas, with the china cups
and saucers I'd set as a girl for tea. The rest
she must have offered my brothers, then turned
her back on that life, emptied out and tired.
I never stopped to think of her then, turning.
It seemed another thing she could manage,
allowing its details to consume her
till she was done to face the future, finished.

*

Remember the day in sharp sunlight
by the pool of their clubhouse:
her face sweating, mottled, the pores
pronounced, her lips quivering,
I said, Mom, are you worried.
She couldn't speak, her eyes
began to glaze, to go flat.
She wanted me to swim laps.
I jumped in but a nagging
sense of her kept me from letting
go in the water –
I took her arm, we inched back
to the building's steps – was it later?
or before that we sat down
at the kitchen table? I took out cards
and shuffled them, gave each of us
a deck of fifty-two to begin
the match. But the woman who
taught me the game just stared.

*

She only worsened that night,
staring at the receiver I handed her
when Luba, then Marion called.
I should have understood the lapse
was a beginning, but instead I tended
to her talking, trying to make her
comfortable, unhooked her enormous
bra, smoothed her sheets, made her
lie down. Even when darkness fell
and she gave out, and her flesh
became a mass of weight, cold then
hot then wet, so heavy I couldn't
turn her to clean the bed – and all
of this as Dad slept and groaned
and wakened to sigh and avert
his eyes from our new truth.
I should have been alarmed, or was I?
As I busied myself with her care,
was there a warning I couldn't hear?

*

Isn't there another way to read a face
brain-stroked, arteries clogged?
to move the palm over its surface like braille
and listen to familiar curves of tone,
press the throat as it warbles in a watery ripple,
release the need to interpret illness
as proof of the way life's lived?

*

Look, she's sleeping now,
her glasses on the table
next to a phone. But she can't
answer. Her words snag.
When I ask if she's sad,
a tear forms in the corner
of her eye. She can no longer
see the field of pine trees
where he took me. Then
her x-ray vision perceived
the world illicit: soldiers
in uniform, secret convocations
near the pavilion, he and I
alone, unseen, though I felt
her gaze upon us where we lay.
Now she's safe in bed,
slowly dying. And he's
there still, a shade
at the end of a woods, alive.

*

I'm not home, my mother
lies in a bed in South
Florida, mucous leaks
from her dried out mouth,
her lungs labor shallow
as a crab, as a bellows
in brief performance.
I sit next to her listening,
no longer wait for her rhythms
to swing from my behavior,
freed of the burden to play out
approval or alleviate pain
by suppressing the self
as it surfaces hot staccato
at family reunions. Still I
want to know what my brother
whispers to open her eyes,
what words he croons
into her ears to soothe her.

*

Oh the habit of acquisition
still numbs the guilt, and as you're leaving
I'm still shopping, still repeating "stop"
as I grab all my hands can hold
before closing time.
I try on sweaters over my t-shirt,
dresses over my pants,
claim I'm buying them for
my daughters when it's me
in the dressing room gorging myself.
Have I neglected you?
taking off in the middle of thought
as you lie still, one ear turned towards me
like an eye? We're both pretending
you're too sick to see through me.
I spend too much money
and wound you again.
This time I promise for what it's worth
to return home empty.

*

In the Vitas Hospice House
on the hospital's 4th floor,
it's always 'after,' what else
is there to do? Yet it hums
with a soft 'before,' tiptoeing
in the halls, till a visitor intrudes,
"one sec, I'll leave you alone –"
but I don't want to talk.
She ropes me into conversation,
brings in her friend
the 'Jewish Priest of Healing'
whose mother in the next room
"has already begun her journey."
My brother and I find ourselves
listening as we follow them,
allow these women
to lay hands on our mother's
chest, to rub her scalp
and praise her readiness –

*

Morning again. The sun shines
on her face, she breathes, sweats,
twitches her mottled feet as I check
them, appears after all these days
on the brink of recovery. Maybe their
priestly hands held power. Or she -
skeptical as ever - found a way
to escape them.
What is our part in this production?
Like a chorus around her bed
we watch each sacred scene
without resistance, and maybe
he's right - how can we do this?
how can we hasten her end
by making her light, assist her lift-off
as the 'priest' applauds her mission,
blesses our skill in letting go –
my brother accused me of murder.

*

She opened her eyes as he repeated
"– for the kids, the kids, the kids!"
As she closed them I said, "She opened
her eyes, she heard, how lucky we are!"
as if to offer him a line through grief.
At the end of seven days he raged.
It was like the scum when soup boils,
an overflow to be wiped away
before serving. Throughout her year-
long illness and stroke-death dying,
I considered her muteness a fitting reply
to his crazed and cursed eruptions:
not to hear them again, or take his
rebukes. I didn't know how he needed
the release till I filled his freezer,
cooked a nourishing stew in preparation
for my leaving. Then I watched him
scream, heard him blame me,
saw my mother's face, her eyes opening.

*

Was that you, Ma, really, at the end? I don't
mean the first time I accustomed my eyes
to the corridor lined with wheelchairs,
afghans and shrunken figures leaning to one side,
their white hair tight against the pinkish scalps
or sticking out in punk-like spikes, and spotting
you at the very end in your new smock
I started running to surprise you, imagining how
you'd smile, when from the side a tiny voice
called my name as I ran by. I turned and recognized
your patient face, your new voice that waited
till we were alone to accept my help, the first time
you said yes, when I asked should I come.
The face of the self-effacing is the hardest to see.
In the end those human sounds must be released,
need to be seen. I mean later, when it seemed
you were silent, beat, gone, and your ears kept on
as your body gave out, they refused to close down
till you'd let each one of us in, safe in sound.

*

I've told the story of her dying enough times now
to establish variations according to skylight, dust
storms, luncheon conversation. In the artificial glow
of an artist's studio I describe my father's rampage
at the end, someone calls it a regression to my
childhood. To break a silence riding home, I tell
my brother's joke from the limousine and everyone
laughs. Over soup I offer a friend the scaled-down
detailed narrative, my role as interpreter illumined
by my brother's need to confess. The friend
caresses my cheek. Years ago he entered my study,
spilled his coffee, kissed me hard. It frightened me
then, I kept on running. Today I turn to face him,
grateful and alarmed. My mother's face in the window
is finally resting. She always napped in the afternoon.
It was all she needed to return her earnings,
investing the smallest tasks with the same concentration
as her noblest plans, their perplexing and elusive
energy slipping from her hands as she ironed each
square white handkerchief and folded it with care.

*

I called every relative I could think of,
even the stingy and self-satisfied ones
my father ridicules and leans on, I wanted
to thank them, to be like mother in that way.
I wrote notes to the condolence card senders
and the ones who prepared food. That's
like her, too, to be grateful, not tardy
with apt expressions. Soon I'll prepare a meal
for my mother's best friend's daughter
who was for Mom all that a lady should be,
in cashmere suits and smiles that light
a room. We went on a trip once, Wendy
and her mom Sue, Aunt Nat and Saralee,
Mom and me. I remember a dressing room
and nothing fit. Mom wanted to admire me
the way Sue beamed as Wendy
emerged glowing. How could I tell her
such excursions filled me with loathing
for all I was, all she wanted of me?

*

Why didn't I bring a sweater? It's cold here,
I should remember, I'm afraid to stop for any
physical discomfort. I want to see my leap
as she perceived it, her warning as I ran outside,
his motor running. Did she envision a future crash,
a marriage interrupted by news of the missing,
headlights searching for signs? She knew I was reckless,
that I entered his car, enclosed her unheeded alarm
in a place only I might come back to, sorry.
Am I? Now that she's gone, he's gone, and the day
returns stark and sunny, nothing else so total
as the memory of her face in consternation, set
against a window as I'm off to embark on sorrow.
But it was never like that, I never loved him as I
love the man I married, never thoughtlessly gave
him my hand or rejected her rule that what we have
must be preserved. I only acted against her premise
a woman must freeze the heat inside her, and
freed it with kisses, near a mountain, in the car, cold.

*

Four weeks have passed now, the details
no less blurred or clear than on that Tuesday
when her breathing eased, her temperature steadied
and it seemed, as always in those frames
of family event, it would go on that way forever.
Till her eyes opened, her heart expanded and
then ceased to beat. Yesterday I received a copy
of her yearbook portrait and quickly
framed it and set it out for all to see.
Whenever someone passed they asked, who?
then, could it be you? that is, me? and of course
it couldn't, the hair soft in thirties style
around the face, the eyes dreamy, composed,
urgent only in their after-fact, when acceptance
comes to mean response to love, disappointment,
and the power of her knowledge then was its vast
contentment. Yet I was stirred by the question.
I quickened at the thought of looking like her,
at friction giving way to this resemblance.

*

Dear mother gone into the rocking
earth the planet unfathomed
Dear mother heaving no longer
from lungs we suctioned cruelly
as if it mattered. Oh Mom, while
we cheered 'good! good!'
we couldn't bear
the god-given order.
Yet we let the act persist,
consulting rabbis to sanction our
behavior. At the end, your face
framed by your whitened hair,
your luminous skin against
the pillow, gave a yellowish tint
to the bleached and ironed linens.
Your bones seemed to rise, your lines
erase. Your calm agreement never
altered, you would not complain.

*

One day maybe I'll come here and let
myself sleep. Bring a mattress and blanket
and cover myself in this room where no
matter what time, I sink tired, weary,
rocking myself to think, like worshippers
in *shul* who close their eyes and sway
to stay awake to the prayer on their lips.
If I lie down maybe she'll join me from
her invisible landing, if she turns the dirt
will sift around her arms and coat her lids.
I'll wipe them as I did those quiet hours
her skin thinned to tissue, gauze and airy
wrappings I didn't recognize. Now I know
the glory of those pauses, dabbing Vaseline
to moisten sores, trying to heal them
as another gesture crossed her openings.
She was marked – how did I miss it? –
by the hand of visiting forces. My eyes
intent upon her couldn't see it.

*

So the concentrated mourning days are past:
your body that released you as I watched
the room fill with soft light, the pillow
that supported your last turning to peer out
on this shrinking world – our eyes –
before you eased away, the dark liquid
that encrusted your lungs with its sticky film
and erupted from the hole that was your mouth,
your voice that seemed to fall and break
like a tiny bird that soothed and then was stopped
in mid-flight, all these have accompanied me
the three months since your death.
And what has emerged in this new region of no
choice and no return is a knowledge of your
deepening, widening life. Like roots
sprouting from the wooden box
where you lie, reaching down, stretching
outward, new perceptions of you
appear on this black and polished slate.

*

In a painting by Francis Bacon called
"Head," a man whose face is erased
takes up a fraction of the canvas. He's
locked inside a booth with a light bulb
glaring through it, burning out his brain
and memory, melting his sweaty flesh.
When my father entered the Sunniland Bank
he had a mourner's beard of thirty days
and wanted me to see it. That's why
he needed their Polaroid camera
reserved for official business. They agreed
to shoot the old man once, then Dad
was off to shave and back before the clerk
could leave for lunch. In the first shot
he's distant, the gray-white whiskers
give him dignity, his jacket's zipped
halfway. The second one's closer, his
mouth gaping in mid-loss, his glasses
a glare, his head hollowed away.

*

The lines are moving away from mother –
thirty days have brought me to a harbor
I see her drifting into distance but no longer
try to stop her. It's enough to be near her
as she rests on the water, to wave and
watch her offer to the ducks that wade
beside her and nibble from her fingers
crumbs I packed for her last outing.

*

Nineteen lines don't comprise a sonnet or
sestina, or invite equal partners in rhyme
or weave into symmetrical song or permit
sweet license to take over and dismiss its
government. Still, it seems a bearable
restriction where enclosure in a convent
would be as fitting, in a country of stone
walls and oaths of silence. But no one really
knows my crimes unless they read my poems.
And the beauty of that disguise is no one
believes the truth of their telling.
So conforming to the laws of man that
guard the gates of female strays is a task
I'll tackle as I seek to know my soul, and
the nineteen lines like a parable in the forest
where rabbis stroll in search of fire-wood
and slowly learn relinquishing of need till
their words are enough, then only vowels
linked through smoke then ash then dust.

*

When the sexual life in a house
subsides, or we go to bed late
and his hand is a wire churning,
pushing into me as though
I were a lamp exposed, filament
broken, ornament torn,
and the heat that would suffice for
light sickens, still the morning
comes, it does. I forget the power
of night to destroy, and the quiet
strength of day. Again his
callused hands surprise, there is
no end to so urgent a force as my
inconstancy, or so violent a project
as this healing from the scraping,
enduring the bruise of these
attacks on a childhood idea
of union, or the grownup
failure to end a girlish wish.

*

Why did I leave exactly at the hour
his secretary said he would call.
I wasn't working well in my study.
I'm afraid of desperately needing
to tell him my heart. Why? In that
other world where my mother lived
such acts performed in place of
speech. I courted her disapproval
in the form of lovers, as her face
would set against me and their arms
restored my will. But him, now?
Turning away I prevent the start
of a new erosion, the earth a mound
covering her flesh, first perfection
since I'm grown I haven't dishonored.
So old habits can be broken, I'm
trying to say, when a mother goes.
Or not thinking deference I observe
resistance, cannot imagine another fall.
In desperation, I remain a patient girl.

*

I'm wondering why I thought I had
to protect you. Why when you asked
I assumed you didn't want to know.
Why I never implored your soothing
voice when it might have comforted.
If I had, could it have opened
new passages to your brain, your heart?
Instead the veins became clogged
then closed. If I'd sought your succor,
your mothering might have served
to eclipse my otherness,
when our differences surfaced
you could have offered a wider view.
But when you called I always lifted
my tone to cheer you, I can't know
what you'd have said if I confessed.
And maybe, just maybe, these are
the wrong questions, there was
nothing more to say, I heard you true.

*

The last time I came here was before
New York, before the leaves started falling,
before Dad died. It's the first I'm telling you,
not that I thought you would break,
you were always strong. And not that you
didn't expect it before your stroke, the first one
when I was there and he wouldn't look,
could barely cope with the new arrangement.
After the third, when you were settled in that
home, he began to serve you like a guard
to be sure they bathed and turned you,
cleaned your nails, kept you upright
in the chair. He became the vigilant
watchdog to unravel years of harm. Once
pointing to his heart you seemed to ask
Are you alright? and moved him to tears.
Not that he didn't cry nonstop, but if you
asked, you cared, that's what he heard.
Let's go home your new voice choked and
turning in disbelief he cried again. "If only
you were well, if you could walk, relieve
yourself, I would!" then he turned away.
Don't you think I want to? were the words
he remembered last, the ones echoing
in the end, when you called him back.

*

Seven months after your death he
followed. It wasn't like when you died,
each of us there, holding your hands,
observing details of decline, trying to arrest
your flight. I'd seen him ten days before,
our ritual fight came early, so the days
remaining we filled with food and walks,
voices soft when we talked about you.
He was counting the days till your birthday
like an impending execution, dreading
the date's red marking as a sign in blood.
After I left he must have made a pact
he couldn't speak of, that the day would
never come. Then you appeared and spoke
to him in dream, forgiving and young.
Maybe I'm telling you things you already
know. What you said he wouldn't tell.
Maybe he started living after your visit
because within a few days he was gone,
quick like he promised, neat and finished
on the floor. No one came to revive
him, it was later we reached the door.

*

We stood before your stone, and since
Dad's isn't carved yet it seemed you were
there alone. He was listening, I suppose,
though all I could hear was the Buffalo cold.
It frosted my face and left you shimmering.
Michael spoke, his function now, as if
our sentiments were shared, but really he stole
the show. As we took off for Miami, the plane
shook, Steve and Michael prayed, we laughed
at how our movement in unison would please you.
When we reached your place I sifted my way
through jewelry, boxes of jewelry, nail clippers, pins
quickly pocketed a few. Mike went through the mail,
Steve dumped drawers of goods. But what led
to the blowup was a photo each of us wanted
of our family posing happy after a fight.
No one budged till Michael stormed outside.
In the course of the night we pooled our loot,
forgave and divvied it up again, siblings afraid
to hold a grudge or carry bitterness ahead.

*

I've invited them all in here:
the ones you suspected I slept with
and a few I kept out of view,
even the silent one and the rogue
who made it hard to leave Buffalo
then never showed up when you
died. You always thought I stole him
from a friend, you thought the worst
of me, I know, I gave you cause.
It's what we had between us,
but did I have to lie –
why couldn't we talk, or fight it out
in the open, or at least try
instead of burying us both alive –
now we're at this party together
you and me and the shades of all
my men, the muses of my sleep,
the fabric of my shroud, the prizes
I earned and hid, to keep your love.

3

THEFTS OF INHERITANCE

These are not the measured urgings of
the first death: seven months she faded
and filled the empty skies of my faraway
home with tiny lights for me to steer by.
Each morning I could remember what
direction shimmered the night before,
what intensity it fathomed, where to take
the conversation suddenly recalled.

Now he lies next to her in the cool ground,
he no longer coughs up phlegm or waits
for my call or worries why my voice is faint
or assumes I've misused the charge card
to enlarge the monster debt he couldn't abide.
None of it beats in him, the drum that
kept him alive, none of it matters to him
anymore, and perhaps that is the new
constellation – to find my way out there
without a parent's knowledge, or
the thefts of inheritance weighing me down.

SNAKE

The belt slipped off my waist and
soundlessly fell to the pavement
as I ran with the child to reach the theater
before a film started.

Only back at the Convalescent Home visiting Mom
and giving Dad's morning fury time to dissolve
I felt for its binding security

suddenly missing. I retraced my steps,
got inside the car and drove to the parking lot
where, from a distance, like a snake

coiled before me waiting
the belt I'd worn at least as long
a time as a man was gone
lay sprawled intact.

Looking back I wondered why space
always sliced this way,
before the cut that silenced me
and after its stunning blow.

How little we know. Now my mother's dead
and the raging father's done
and the belt that seemed a necessary charm
is hardly worn.

But the man who left is back smiling
from wherever he's been.

He always made a lot of noise

like the clerk at the post office whose
involvement in everyone's cause
holds up the line and gets on my nerves
till one day I see tears just under
the surface and recall how Dad, eyes
brimming, asked questions in every
direction: always ready to serve,
tie-clip winking "business is terrific,"
cigar stub hanging from his mouth,
the Peter Falk wrinkled trench coat
billowing around; even in winter, ice
underfoot, the big man never dressed
warm enough, the salesman whose luck
had turned carried gifts to our grownup
rooms and we refused his offerings:
"just trying to do good –" he said,
searching out deals, blowing
his nose, returning surplus junk
from the old garage; he greeted
stock-boys as his friend, overflowed
with praise when a waiter was polite –
that noisy bawling man hasn't
made a sound since September.

ORPHAN

He died so soon after her, I can't be
sure I ever touched the edge of his hair,
or the age spot brown on his cheek,
or even held him clear in mind.
Happy is the orphan whose father's
yearnings block out memory! *Happy*
is the orphan whose mother's gaze
remains unmoved! My mother and
father sleep in a grave so deep I
tried to fathom them, and nearly fell
inside, bending over the edge I couldn't
reach their end, they were alive,
I want to define it, not to mistake
this sigh for a single rapturous cry.

FEED THE ENEMY

It's afraid, too.
Bring it close,
open its wet mouth.

It's through sex we express
whatever it is, he said.

If it's hungry it attacks,
leaving scraps on the rug.

Neither bad nor good,
these claws, these snarling
coils:

his scent in the dark furrow

the wish that arouses
hope

to spark
like a live wire

grounded in
doubt
(in recognition)

I'll become whole
by cutting apart

SNOW

All night the snow fell and I didn't think
of either man, not the one I lost who came back
this week smiling, not the one I pursued
whose body sleeps under blankets in another
country in another whiteness, I was blank
as night, empty of longing, a snow-filled
garden all at rest, dormant, not dead,
without struggle, without weeping,
cold as the clean air, quiet as snow falling.

The children are here, every one of them
asleep in this house, the roof holding
half a meter of new snow, Jerusalem
covered and old as tradition, no political
tension today as the fighters throw snow
and laugh and aim at trees whose branches
are heavy with wet flakes, all night
falling, all night watching, lighting.
And as they sleep I'll return as their mother,

I'll wake myself from this journey out
of my given life, return as their shelter
because when I'm away as anyone else
trampling the newly fallen snow with my
scarf around my neck, my eyes squinting
to see the objects ahead of me, I'm no
one looking into windows to see her reflection,
to find which knob fits her hand,
what step to climb and claim as my own.

It doesn't matter anymore he stopped
speaking to me when his marriage

was threatened by our talking, and with one
step he took two, the silent cut
more shocking than the first turning
meant years and years of snow falling,
I would walk inside, see nothing
but his face in the whiteness, for in
some miraculous way it came clearer

through the storm, I learned its features
in absence, the stark outline of his fear
as I needed to see him to save my
sanity unfolded into comfort and ease,
his, I mean to say, because he
adjusted to the stricture with a kind
of delight, and when we met the other
morning, kisses on cheeks and no one
apparently affected by what had happened

I understood he stopped thinking of me
after a while, accustomed to family
realigned, the hole I'd filled painted over,
covered with a thin film like snow,
or a negative repaired with glue, or
a child's skin healing, the fall forgotten.

BEFORE MEMORY

I was a bell
I rang though no one could hear
I was the movement
in time
I made myself small

I was a bell and I was small
with a tiny voice
I rang in time
behind everything
I rang and rang

almost inaudibly
but I was there
as though all the ringing
that could not be heard
had a resonance

without which
there was no music
no meaning
or form
to the days' passing.

FIELD NOTES

Now I know why I came here:
to open a wound

where skin had healed
on a spot still tender from earlier bruisings.

And it's always through
pleasure the tissue thickens,

soon I may stand erect
a perfect survivor

my body covered with medals
flayed, pink, raw.

RETREAT

You go deep into daylight
bleaching out the stains
of our encounter
that grow faint as you fuel
the self you need to be,
the one whose hands rub
and scrape, letting go of me.

A SEXUAL ATTRACTION

I won't concede, he said,
but will revel in your
concession.

She came to him
under his conditions.

That he traveled far
to meet her
seemed a suspension
of the terms,
another center of feeling.

Whenever they met
he renewed the contract
through silence and
distancing,
speech cold and scientific,

each time she remembered
too late, after his
lips had blazed
and branded her

that he meant what he said
no matter how
they burned

he'd give only his word
to comfort her.

AIRMAIL

A child
I fumbled in the dust
my fingers white and plump
inside the crumpled bag
till I reached rectangles
and square
after square
of thin airmail sheets
and on them your
familiar script,
the strips you licked
now ripped edges like the cliff
I once
jumped off in celebration
of separation.
I thought I'd suffocate
breathing them in again.
I opened one and then
another and around me
they fell like clouds
soft and gentle
as your voice had been.
Too late to return
to that city where I left you
writing letters,
how can I tell you
what I've learned?

NOTE

The phrase "Happy is the orphan" (in the poem "Orphan") is adapted from Sholem Aleichem's unfinished novel *Motl the Cantor's Son*.